D0854816

© 1990 Franklin Watts

Franklin Watts Inc
387 Park Avenue South
New York NY 10016

Printed in Belgium

Designed by
K and Co

Photographs by
NASA
JPL
TASS
Mat Irvine
Hale Observatory
Lowell Observatory
European Space Agency

Technical Consultants
L. J. Carter
S. Young

Library of Congress Cataloging-in-Publication Data

Barrett, Norman S.
     The picture world of space voyages / Norman Barrett.
        p.   cm. — (Picture World)
     Summary: Examines the various manned and unmanned missions into
space and describes their discoveries.
     ISBN 0-531-14057-1
     1. Astronautics—Juvenile literature. 2. Outer space—
—Exploration—Juvenile literature. [1. Astronautics. 2. Outer
space— Exploration.] I. Title. II. Series.
TL793.S736 1990
523.2—dc20   89-21539
                                                                       CIP AC

The Picture World of

Space Voyages

N. S. Barrett

CONTENTS

Franklin Watts

New York • London • Sydney • Toronto

Introduction

Exploring space is the great new adventure of the modern age. Powerful rockets send manned and unmanned spacecraft on voyages to unknown worlds.

Astronauts have landed on the Moon. Space probes have passed close to distant planets such as Jupiter, Saturn and Neptune.

△ The spacecraft Voyager approaches giant planet Jupiter, on its journey through the Solar System.

△ The Soviet space station Mir, together with the scientific module Kvant. More modules were scheduled to be added to Mir, which is now permanently manned and has orbited the Earth since February 1986.

▷ American astronaut Neil Armstrong, the first man on the Moon.

7

Man on the Moon

The first great space expedition was the Apollo mission, which landed the first astronauts on the Moon in 1969.

Before that, Soviet space probes were the first to go around the Moon in 1959. U.S. spacecraft landed on the Moon to test landing sites, and in 1968 took astronauts around the Moon for the first time.

▷ The launch of Apollo 11, which landed the first people from Earth on the Moon.

▽ On an earlier mission, the lunar module orbits the Moon by itself before rejoining the command module. This was a rehearsal for the first Moon landing.

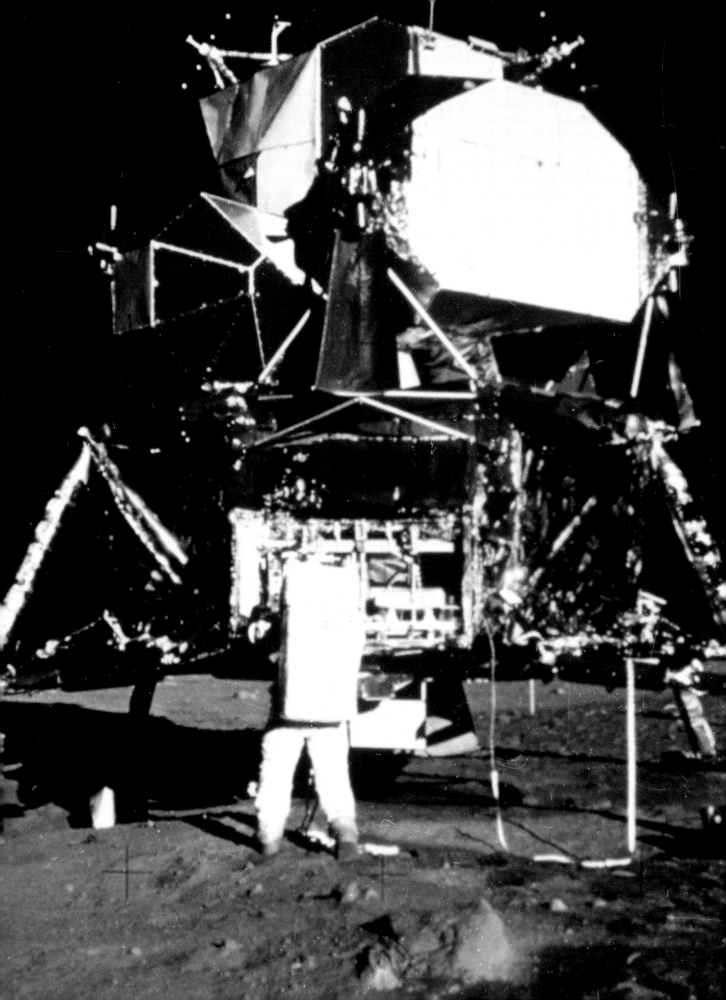

◁ Astronaut Edwin Aldrin is photographed in front of the lunar module after the first successful landing.

△ The last manned landing, Apollo 17, took place in 1972. A lunar roving vehicle is on the right.

▽ A memorable experience for the Apollo astronauts was to see the Earth hovering over the Moon's horizon.

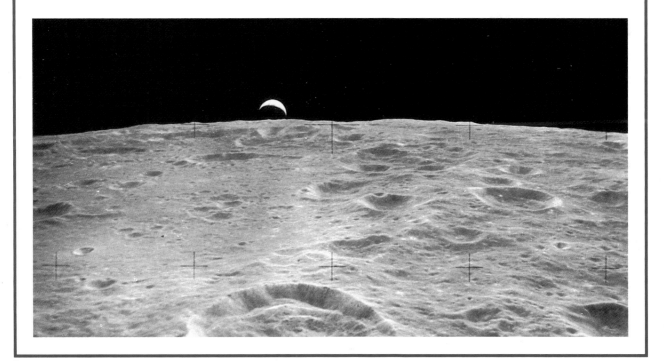

Landing on the Moon was a journey to the unknown. There is no air to breathe and it is intensely hot during the day and freezing cold at night. Astronauts needed to wear special pressurized spacesuits when they left their spacecraft.

The first steps on the Moon's surface were taken very carefully. But the astronauts soon became used to moving around. Because the Moon is so much smaller than the Earth, people on its surface feel much lighter.

▽ A television picture from a camera left on the Moon shows how the astronauts returned. Part of the lunar module, called the ascent stage, is blasted off from the descent stage, which served as a platform. Much less power is needed to break away from the Moon's weaker gravity than from the Earth's.

△ The command module of Apollo 11 over the Moon's surface. One astronaut orbited the Moon in the command module while the others were on the Moon. After they blasted off from the Moon, they docked with the command module. They then set the lunar module free, and returned to Earth.

The various stages of landing on the Moon and returning safely to Earth had been worked out carefully. The methods had been rehearsed as far as possible. But nobody knew for certain how well they would work.

The success of the Apollo mission was a tribute to a whole army of scientists and engineers. It was also due to the skill and courage of the astronauts who took part.

13

Exploring Mars

After their historic landings on the Moon, the Americans concentrated on building space shuttles. Soviet space research focused on keeping cosmonauts in space for long periods of time.

Both the Americans and the Russians began to make plans for landing people on Mars.

Several unmanned probes have been sent to Mars, a journey that takes six months or more. Much information has been sent back.

▽ A Viking probe, one of two U.S. spacecraft that orbited Mars in 1976.

◁ A Viking lander. Landers were parachuted onto Mars and sent back important information about its surface and very thin atmosphere. Experiments failed to detect any signs of life.

▷ The Soviet probe Phobos, one of two sent to study Mars and its planet Phobos in 1989. Phobos 1 was lost because of an error in a command from Earth. Radio contact was mysteriously lost with Phobos 2, but not before it had sent back vital information and excellent pictures.

15

A permanent settlement on the Moon will probably have to be built before a manned expedition can set out for Mars.

Space agency NASA has outlined plans for a Moon base by the year 2001 and an outpost on Mars some 12 to 15 years later. Astronauts would stay on the planet for about two years before returning to Earth.

▽ How a robotic rover will look on Mars. There are plans to land such a vehicle on the planet in the late 1990s. Samples of soil, rock and atmosphere will be collected and sent back to Earth.

Into the unknown

All space voyages involve venturing into the unknown. But some are so dangerous that only unmanned spacecraft may be sent.

Venus, Earth's closest neighbor among the planets, hides its secrets behind swirling clouds of deadly acid. Space probes have been sent to study Venus. Some have been orbiting the planet and sending back information for several years. Others have landed, and sent back details of Venus's surface.

△ Halley's comet in 1910. The planet Venus can be seen below, to the left. This best known of comets has been studied at close hand by space probes sent from Earth during its mid-1980's visit to Earth's vicinity.

17

Comets look like fuzzy stars when they appear in the night sky. They travel around the Sun, sometimes taking hundreds or even thousands of years to complete one orbit. They are basically made up of ice and dust, and glow brightly when they come close to the Sun.

In 1985, unmanned space probes were sent out to study Halley's comet, making its first appearance since 1910.

△ A picture of the surface of Venus taken from a Venera lander, part of which can be seen at bottom right.

▷ The spacecraft Giotto on its "suicide" mission into the coma (head) of Halley's comet. It emerged with some damage but kept sending signals. Several other probes were sent up to study the comet from a distance.

Swinging around the planets

Some of the most exciting space voyages have been made by unmanned spacecraft visiting several planets in turn. This has been made possible by using the gravity of one planet to "fling" the spacecraft in slingshot fashion towards another.

The Voyager 2 spacecraft, launched in 1977, visited four of the outer planets in 12 years.

▽ The Voyager 2 spacecraft visited Jupiter in 1979, Saturn in 1981, Uranus in 1986 and Neptune in 1989. It was equipped with cameras and instruments to record information and transmit it back to Earth.

Unmanned spacecraft sent to study the Solar System (the Sun and the planets) do not return to Earth.

Some continue orbiting a planet or are allowed to crash onto it. Other probes are left to orbit the Sun. Some spacecraft, such as Pioneer 10 and the two voyager probes, leave the Solar System altogether.

△ An artist's impression of the Galileo space probe orbiting Jupiter, with the moon Io on the left. Sent up in 1989, Galileo is expected to reach Jupiter in 1995.

When spacecraft leave the Solar System, they continue on their journey towards the stars.

No one knows whether there is intelligent life out there — on a planet like Earth, perhaps, orbiting a star like our Sun. But a record of the sounds of Earth was carried on the Voyager spacecraft, including music, whale songs and "hellos" in 60 languages.

△ Neptune, the last planet visited by Voyager 2 on its remarkable voyage around the Solar System. After sending back dramatic pictures of Neptune and its moon Triton, and discovering six new moons, Voyager began to head for interstellar space.

Space stations

Space stations are set up in Earth's orbit with living and working quarters for scientists. They are long-term projects intended to be manned all the time, with a regular change of crew.

The Russians set up the first permanent space station, Mir, in 1986. Manned and unmanned spacecraft dock with Mir.

▽ Space station Freedom, as planned by NASA. Space shuttle missions in the late 1990s are scheduled to build and service this huge orbiting laboratory, which might also serve as a staging post for manned flights to the Moon or Mars.

Journey to the stars

The spacecraft, or starship, that takes people to worlds outside our Solar System will have to be propelled by something more powerful than rocket fuel.

A space shuttle traveling at top speed would take 160,000 years to reach the nearest star. Scientists believe it will be possible to build an unmanned spacecraft sometime in the next century capable of getting there in 35 years.

▷ Light from the stars takes years to reach us on Earth. Even if able to travel at about an eighth of the speed of light, a spacecraft could reach only a few of the nearest stars in a human lifetime.

▽ A model of a spacecraft designed to travel at an eighth of the speed of light – propelled by a series of nuclear explosions.

Facts

Voyage to Venus
The first object from Earth to reach the surface of another planet was the Soviet spacecraft Venera 3. The Venera probes were a series of spacecraft sent out to study Venus. Venera 3 crashed onto the planet in 1966.

Space Pioneer
The first spacecraft to fly by Jupiter was Pioneer 10, in 1973, on its way to becoming the first object from Earth to leave the Solar System.

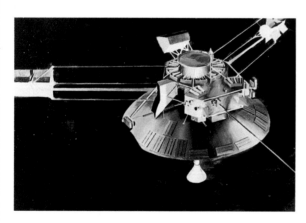

△ Pioneer 10, the first spacecraft to leave the Solar System.

Twelve men on the Moon
The six successful Apollo missions to land men on the Moon resulted in 12 astronauts actually walking on its surface.

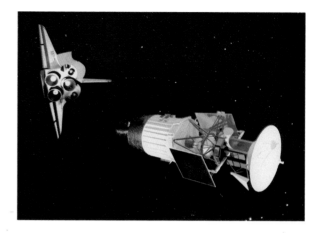

△ The space probe Magellan is launched on its way to Venus from the Atlantis shuttle.

Magellan's new mission
In May 1989 the space shuttle Atlantis launched a spacecraft called Magellan on its 15-month journey to the planet Venus. It was the first launch of an interplanetary probe from a shuttle.

Magellan's mission is to map Venus. It is named after Ferdinand Magellan, the Portuguese sea captain who, in the 1500s, led the first expedition to sail completely around the world.

Light-years
A light-year is a measure of distance. It is the distance traveled by light in one year.

This is a distance of about 10 trillion km (6 trillion miles). The nearest stars are over 4 light-years away.

Riding to Mars on sunbeams

The 500th anniversary of Christopher Columbus's first voyage to the Americas falls in 1992. A U.S. government commission, set up to commemorate this historic event, is sponsoring three spacecraft – from Europe, Asia and America – in a "race" to Mars. The three craft, named Nina, Pinta and Santa Maria, after Columbus's fleet, will be propelled by solar energy after being launched by rocket into a high Earth orbit. The pressure of particles of sunlight on their huge "sails" should then push them to Mars in about a year.

Galileo, by Jupiter!

In October 1989 the space probe Galileo was launched from the shuttle Atlantis. It is named after the Italian astronomer and scientist who discovered the four major moons of Jupiter in 1610.

After swinging around Venus and the Earth on its six-year, 4,000 million km (2,500 million mile) voyage to Jupiter, Galileo will parachute a science probe onto the raging atmosphere of the giant planet. Galileo itself will make a close study of Jupiter and the moons first seen nearly 400 years earlier by the famous astronomer.

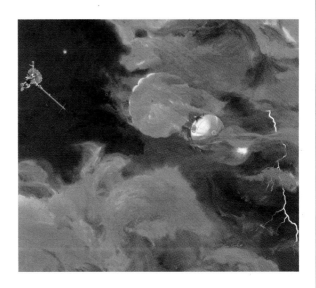

△ An artist's impression of a science probe parachuting into Jupiter's atmosphere from Galileo (shown top left). The probe is scheduled to send back information for 75 minutes before it is crushed by the atmosphere's pressure.

Glossary

Dock
To join up in space. Spacecraft or parts of spacecraft can dock with each other or with a space station.

Gravity
The attraction that one body exerts on another. Gravity is why things "fall" to the ground. The lighter the body, the less gravity – or gravitational pull – it has.

Interstellar
Between the stars.

Lander
The part of a spacecraft landed on the Moon or a planet.

Lunar
Having to do with the Moon.

Module
A detachable part of a spacecraft used for a special purpose, or a section added to a space station.

Orbit
The path taken in space by one body moving around another. The force of gravity between the two bodies keeps the lighter one in orbit. We also say that one body "orbits" another.

Slingshot
A method for accelerating spacecraft through the Solar System by using the gravity of the planets.

Solar System
The Sun and its planets and their moons, together with all the space that comes under the Sun's influence.

Space probe
An unmanned spacecraft whose main purpose is to study planets or other bodies.

Space station
A laboratory in space, orbiting the Earth, with working and living quarters for astronauts and scientists. Space stations will be regularly visited by spacecraft from Earth with supplies and replacement crew.

Index

PRINTED IN BELGIUM BY
proost
INTERNATIONAL BOOK PRODUCTION